Women in STEM

LIFE SCIENCE

Edited by Jane Dunne

LIGHTBOX
openlightbox.com

LIGHTBOX

Go to
www.openlightbox.com
and enter this book's
unique code.

ACCESS CODE

LBXJ3269

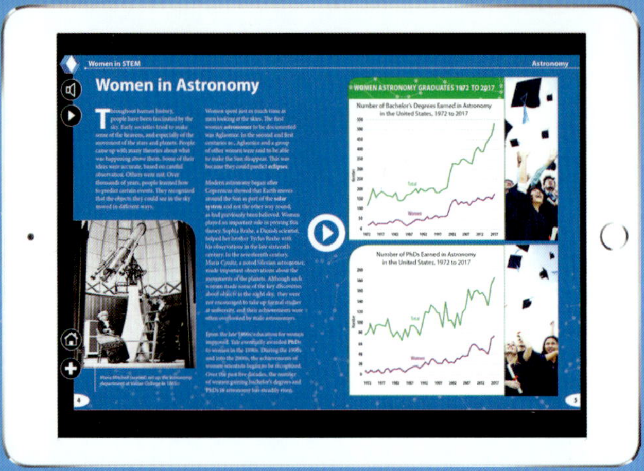

Lightbox is an all-inclusive digital solution for the teaching and learning of curriculum topics in an original, groundbreaking way. Lightbox is based on National Curriculum Standards.

STANDARD FEATURES OF LIGHTBOX

AUDIO High-quality narration using text-to-speech system

ACTIVITIES Printable PDFs that can be emailed and graded

SLIDESHOWS Pictorial overviews of key concepts

VIDEOS Embedded high-definition video clips

WEBLINKS Curated links to external, child-safe resources

TRANSPARENCIES Step-by-step layering of maps, diagrams, charts, and timelines

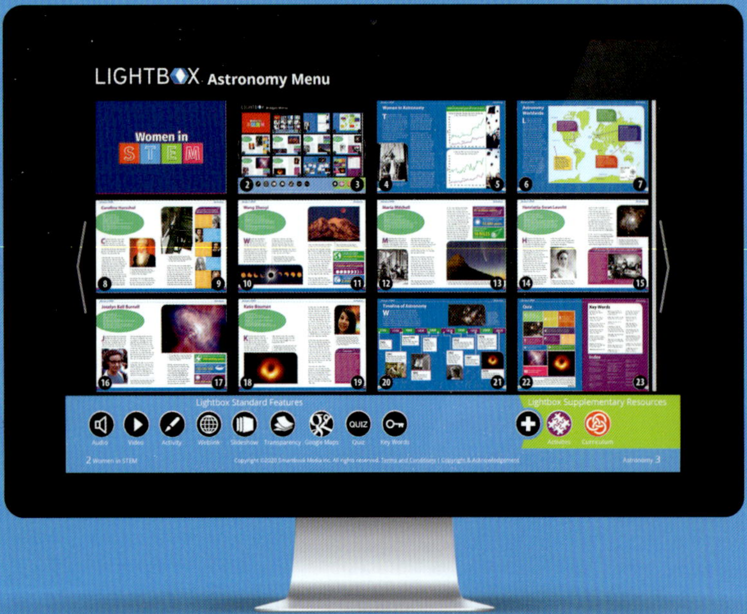

INTERACTIVE MAPS Interactive maps and aerial satellite imagery

QUIZZES Ten multiple choice questions that are automatically graded and emailed for teacher assessment

KEY WORDS Matching key concepts to their definitions

Women in STEM

LIFE SCIENCE

CONTENTS

Women in Life Science

The study of life science has many branches. Zoologists study animals, botanists study plants, and paleontologists study organisms that became extinct millions of years ago. **Geneticists** look at how animals and plants inherit characteristics from their parents. Biochemists examine the molecules that make up all living things.

Living things exist in **ecosystems**. If one **species** becomes extinct, other species in the ecosystem suffer. An important part of life science is ecology, or the study of the environment.

Ecologists study ecosystems, and the relationship between the natural world and human activity. For centuries, scientists worked to grow better plants and raise bigger animals, without thinking about how human needs were affecting the planet. Today, **conservationists** work to protect the natural world.

In Europe, women were involved in life sciences from the start of modern science in the 1550s. In 1699, the German **naturalist**, Maria Sibylla Merian, traveled to South America to study insects. She wrote a book about her discoveries.

Zoologists study all types of animals. One area of research is to report on how agriculture affects the habitats of wild animals.

Frenchwoman Catherine Jérémie collected information about new species she found in Canada. Mary Ann Whitby helped biologist Charles Darwin in his research.

In the early 1900s, many women contributed to the scientific understanding of Earth and all living things. Although many of these women began to study the natural world as a hobby, women have helped to shape the history of life sciences. In the 2000s, many of the world's most respected life scientists are women.

Rachel Carson's book, *Silent Spring*, warned against the use of poisons to kill insects feeding on crops. The book inspired people to think about the environment and how to protect it.

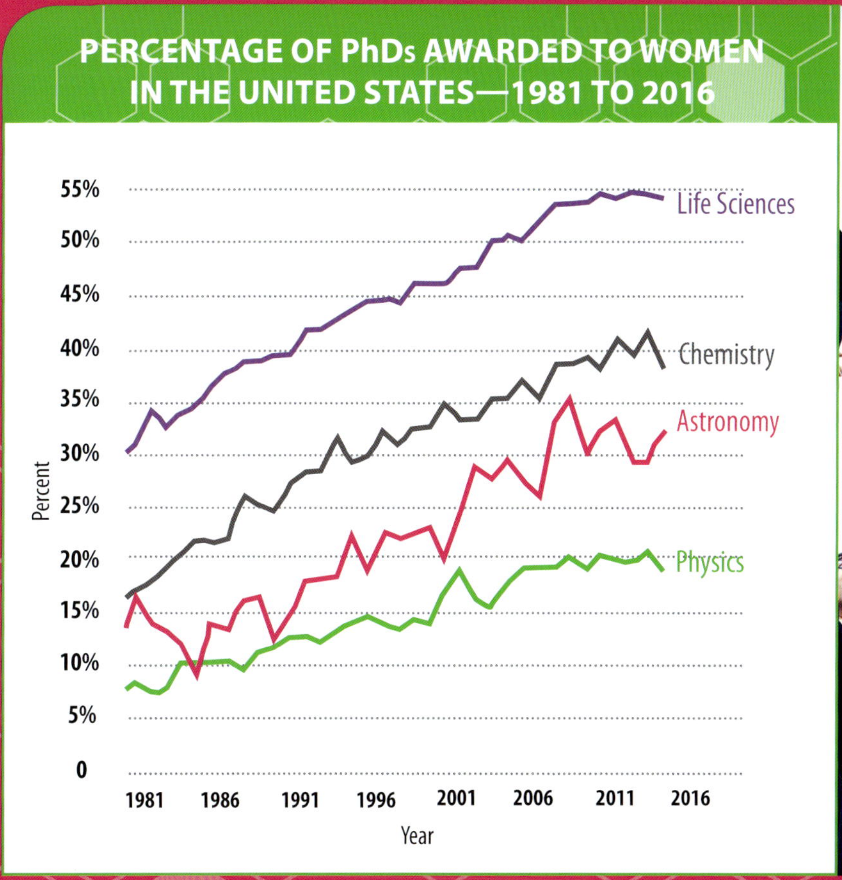

Life Science Worldwide

People have studied animals and plants worldwide for hundreds of thousands of years. Knowledge of what is now called life science was part of the knowledge that ordinary people had in order to survive in poor, rural communities. This knowledge included knowing how to breed animals, and the life cycle of plants through the changing seasons.

In the fifteenth to eighteenth centuries, women researched and cataloged the huge number of different species that were being discovered in the natural world. Women became experts in the study of lichens and fungi. The first skeletons of reptiles from the age of the dinosaurs were discovered. Such discoveries changed the way scientists viewed the world. It seemed that Earth was older than scientists had thought. These discoveries were important arguments supporting Charles Darwin's theory of **evolution**. More recently, women life scientists have led research into global warming and climate change, and the effects these are having on the planet.

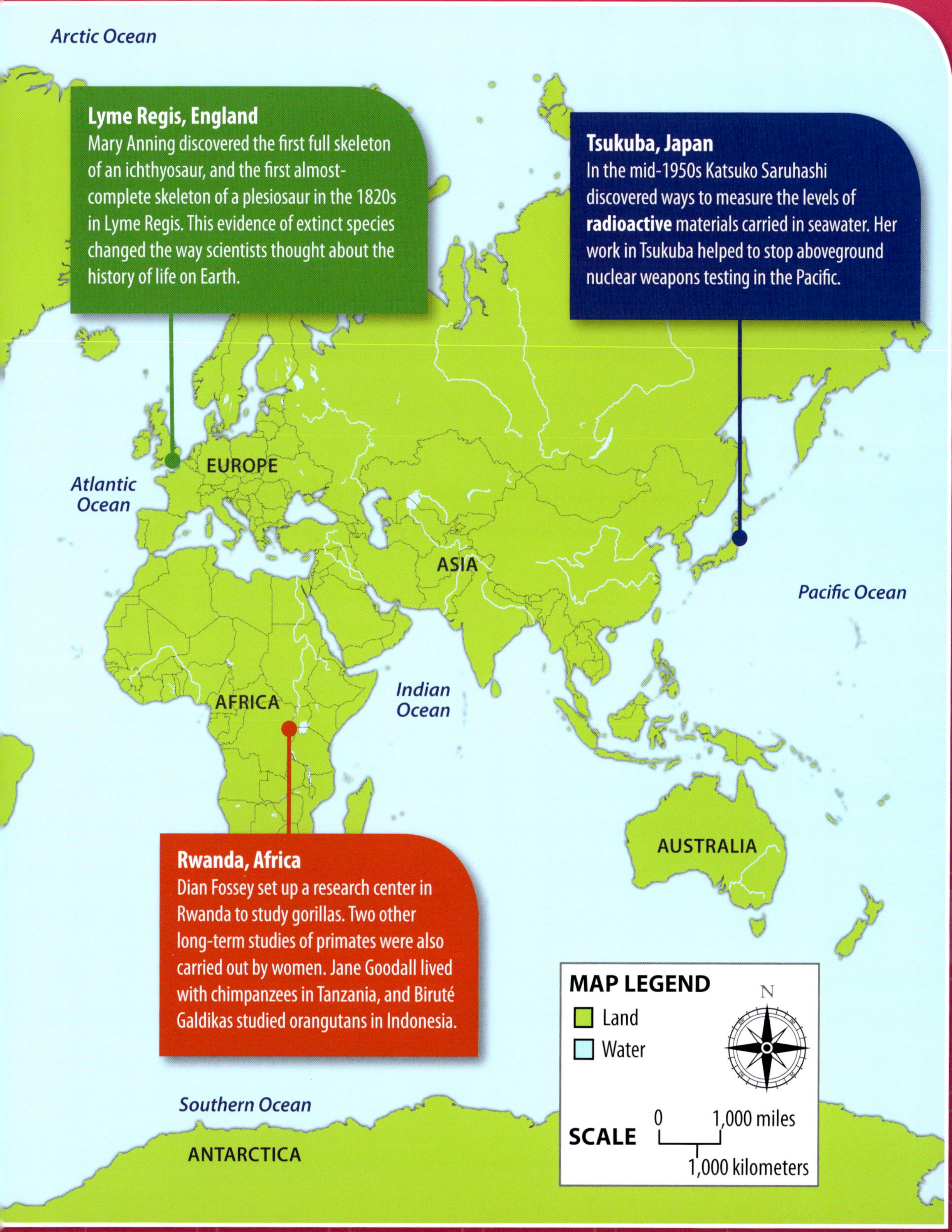

Lyme Regis, England

Mary Anning discovered the first full skeleton of an ichthyosaur, and the first almost-complete skeleton of a plesiosaur in the 1820s in Lyme Regis. This evidence of extinct species changed the way scientists thought about the history of life on Earth.

Tsukuba, Japan

In the mid-1950s Katsuko Saruhashi discovered ways to measure the levels of **radioactive** materials carried in seawater. Her work in Tsukuba helped to stop aboveground nuclear weapons testing in the Pacific.

Rwanda, Africa

Dian Fossey set up a research center in Rwanda to study gorillas. Two other long-term studies of primates were also carried out by women. Jane Goodall lived with chimpanzees in Tanzania, and Biruté Galdikas studied orangutans in Indonesia.

Mary Anning

Name: Mary Anning
Born: 1799, Lyme Regis, Dorset, Great Britain
Died: 1847, Lyme Regis, Dorset, Great Britain
Occupation: Fossil hunter and palaeontologist
Education: Self-taught
Major discoveries and achievements: Skeletons of ichthyosaur, plesiosaur, and pterosaur
Major honors: None in her lifetime. In 2010, Great Britain's top science association, the Royal Society, named her as one of the 10 most influential women in the history of science

Mary was born into a poor family in Lyme Regis, on the south coast of Great Britain. She was one of 10 children, but only Mary and her brother, Joseph, survived to adulthood. Her father was a furniture maker, but he made extra money for the family by collecting objects he found in the chalk cliffs along the beach and selling them to tourists. These objects were **fossils** that were revealed when the chalk cliffs were worn down during winter storms.

At the age of 12, Mary found the most complete fossil of a large reptile that had lived in the sea. This was the ichthyosaur. In 1823, she discovered the skeleton of a sea-living reptile called a plesiosaur. Five years later, she also found the first fossil of a winged reptile, the pterosaur.

The low-lying cliffs of Lyme Regis were formed during the Jurassic period. This was between 200 and 145 million years ago.

Nothing like these creatures had ever been seen before. Most people believed that the world was only a few thousand years old and that living things had not changed over that time. Mary's discoveries showed that different species had once lived on the planet millions of years ago.

Despite her discoveries, many scientists did not treat Mary as an equal because she was a woman. However, she continued to learn about palaeontology and talk to scientists. By the time she died, Mary had finally been recognized as a world expert.

Mary was a familiar sight on the chalk cliffs near Lyme Regis. She carried a basket and a hammer, and was always accompanied by a dog.

"OLD DORSET"

Mary did not feel she had been treated well by other scientists. Although her work was written about in scientific papers, she received no credit. However, her discoveries had an almost instant impact on the world of science.

In 1830, British **geologist** Henry De la Beche painted a picture of the sea creatures and flying reptiles Mary had discovered. He gave it a Latin name meaning "Old Dorset". He added fish, some of which had been found inside the fossils. The painting was reproduced as a print. Palaeontologist William Buckland handed copies out at lectures.

Although Mary had not received recognition or money for her work, she benefitted from the prints. De la Beche sold them to friends for about 2 dollars each. He gave the money to Mary.

De la Beche's painting of ancient creatures was reproduced in science journals all over Europe.

Barbara McClintock

Name: Eleanor "Barbara" McClintock
Born: 1902, Hartford, Connecticut
Died: 1992., Huntingdon, New York State
Occupation: Geneticist
Education: Cornell University
Major discoveries and achievements: Produced the first genetic map of maize
Major honors: National Medal of Science, 1970; Nobel Prize in Physiology or Medicine, 1983

Barbara was baptized Eleanor, but her parents soon decided that her dynamic personality was more suited to the name Barbara. She was a bright, independent child, and did very well at high school. Her teachers encouraged her to go to Cornell University to study **botany** and genetics. Her PhD was in a branch of genetics that studies how **chromosomes** relate to **cell** behavior. This branch of genetics science is called cytogenetics.

Chromosomes can split and make copies of themselves. This is how genes are passed on to the next generation. Barbara used microscopes to identify chromosomes inside cells. She was the first person to describe how chromosomes formed a cross shape. She was also the first person to prove that individual genes could move between chromosomes.

Barbara took up a post at the University of Missouri in 1936. There, she continued her work using x-rays. She realized x-rays could cause **mutations** in chromosomes.

In the 1940s, Barbara McClintock led research studies in the relatively new science of genetics.

The variation in colors in maize plants is caused by the unexpected movement of genes in their chromosomes.

From 1944 onward, Barbara studied maize plants. She discovered that gene mutations caused differences in color by comparing one plant's chromosomes with those of its parent plant. Some of the genes were in different positions. This was a breakthrough in genetics, but it was not taken seriously by other scientists and she stopped publishing her results.

In the 1960s, other geneticists began to appreciate the work Barbara had done. Their experiments confirmed her theories. More than 30 years after she had proposed the theory of "mobile genetic elements," she was awarded the Nobel Prize in Physiology or Medicine.

MILESTONES IN LIFE SCIENCE

Anton van Leewenhoek was one of the first **microbiologists**. In the late 1600s, he made microscopes with lenses that were more powerful than any others at the time. He discovered a world of small creatures and bacteria that was invisible to the naked eye.

Carl Linnaeus was a Swedish botanist and zoologist. He visited Lapland in 1732 and listed all the animals and plants he found there, naming and classifying them. His system of **taxonomy** is still used today.

Charles Lyell was a Scottish geologist. In the 1800s, he wrote a book suggesting that Earth was older than people had thought. His work contributed to Darwin's theories on the processes of evolution.

Charles Darwin went on a voyage around the world the 1830s. In 1859, he wrote *On the Origin of Species,* which put forward the revolutionary theory of evolution by **natural selection**.

Gregor Mendel was a monk who experimented with pea plants in the mid-1800s. He discovered that genes come in pairs. He also showed that a pea plant receives one gene from each parent plant.

Rachel Carson

Name: Rachel Carson
Born: 1907, Springdale, Pennsylvania
Died: 1964, Silver Spring, Maryland
Occupation: Marine biologist, zoologist, writer, and ecologist
Education: Chatham University, Johns Hopkins University
Major discoveries and achievements: Authored *Silent Spring*, a book that went on to spark the modern environmental movement
Major honors: After she died, Rachel Carson was awarded the Presidential Medal of Freedom in 1980.

Rachel Carson grew up in the rural river town of Springdale. She loved the natural world and did well in biology at high school. Rachel was awarded a scholarship to Johns Hopkins University to study for a master's in biology. To earn money to fund her studies, Rachel became a scriptwriter for the U.S. Bureau of Fisheries. She wrote short radio programs about aquatic life, and found she had a gift for making marine biology accessible. In 1952, her book *The Sea Around Us* became a best seller. Rachel described the world's oceans, the animals and plants living in them, and the winds, currents, and tides.

Rachel was now a respected author, but she was becoming increasingly worried by the use of **pesticides** in the United States. These were in widespread use after World War II. One of the first was dichlorodiphenyltrichloroethane, a "wonder chemical" known as DDT.

DDT was first used by the U.S. military to prevent malaria and other diseases during World War II. Farmers also used it on crops to kill pests.

During the 1950s, Rachel carried out her own research for a book on pesticides. In the book, she wrote about the harmful effects of strong pesticides on humans and wildlife, and the long-term damage caused by pesticides once they entered the **food chain**. *Silent Spring* was published in 1962. It immediately caused disagreement. The chemical manufacturers said her research was faulty, but other scientists agreed with her. Rachel's book had a long-lasting effect on the environmental movement of the 1960s. She testified in front of the U.S. Senate to argue for stronger anti-pollution laws. Eight years after Rachel died, DDT was officially banned in the United States.

2,000 million tons (1.8 metric tons) of **DDT** have been **made** since the mid- **twentieth century.**

DDT stays in the **body** more than **6 YEARS** after someone has been exposed to it.

170 countries agreed to ban **DDT** in 2004.

Spraying crops with chemicals not only kills insects on crops, it also soaks into the soil and rivers. Fish and aquatic plants absorb the poison, and birds, such as bald eagles, eat the fish. As a result, the birds produce eggs with such thin shells that they break before the eaglets can hatch.

Dian Fossey

Name: Dian Fossey
Born: 1932, San Francisco, California
Died: 1985, Volcanoes National Park, Rwanda
Occupation: Zoologist, conservationist
Education: San Jose State College, University of Cambridge
Major discoveries and achievements: Establishment of Karisoke Research Center in 1967

Dian Fossey had wanted to become a vet, but she failed her chemistry exams in her second year. Instead, she studied occupational therapy. In the mid-1950s, she worked at the Kosair Crippled Children's Hospital in Louisville, Kentucky. However, Dian had not given up her ambition to work with animals. In 1963, she went on a trip to Africa and heard about the work of Jane Goodall, who was studying chimpanzees by living with them.

Dian Fossey formed a strong relationship with some of the gorillas she studied.

In 1966, Dian returned to Africa. Louis Leakey, a leading researcher of prehistoric humans in Tanzania, had suggested she go and study mountain gorillas. These gorillas live in the mountainous border regions of Rwanda, Uganda, and the Democratic Republic of the Congo (DRC). In 1967, Dian set up camp in the rainforests of Rwanda. At first, she found it difficult to make contact with the gorillas. They were hard to find in the forest, and ran away as soon as they saw humans. Eventually, Dian was able to get close to them by imitating the noises they made, and copying the way they moved.

Dian Fossey lived for decades with her gorillas. She learned how to identify each animal by its unique nose wrinkles.

Dian set up a research center in two small tents and began the study of mountain gorillas that would take up the rest of her life. She led an international campaign to raise public awareness about how gorillas are endangered. Through her work, she showed that gorillas are gentle **herbivores** with a highly developed social structure. She started the Dian Fossey Gorilla Fund to work with local communities and governments. In 1983, Dian wrote about her work in the book *Gorillas in the Mist*. The book was turned into a successful movie in 1988.

In 1984, Dian set up Gorilla Doctors, a group giving veterinary care to wild gorillas. She also worked to stop **poaching**. In 1985, she was killed in her cabin. The crime was never solved, but the Karisoke Research Center continues her work.

JANE GOODALL AND BIRUTÉ GALDIKAS

Two other women also carried out research into wild primates in the twentieth century.

In the 1960s, Jane Goodall spent many years studying the behavior of endangered chimpanzees in the forests of Gombe National Park in Tanzania. She discovered that chimpanzees use tools, are not strictly vegetarian, and have fierce fights.

In the 1970s, Biruté Galdikas began her study of orangutans in Indonesia. She discovered that these apes also use tools. She set up a reserve for orangutans that had been captured as pets and then abandoned. She is a world authority on orangutans.

Jane Goodall revised previous beliefs about the behavior and diet of chimpanzees.

Sylvia Earle

Name: Sylvia Earle
Born: 1935, Gibbstown, New Jersey
Occupation: Oceanographer and explorer
Education: Florida State University, Duke University
Major discoveries and achievements: Chief Scientist at the National Oceanic and Atmospheric Administration, 1990–1992; establishment of Mission Blue, 2009
Major honors: National Audubon Society's Rachel Carson Award, 2009; Hubbard Medal, 2013

As a child, Sylvia was fascinated by nature. She was 12 years old when her family moved to the Florida coast. The salt marshes and sea grass beds around their house gave Sylvia a whole new landscape to explore. After high school, Sylvia went to Florida State University, where she learned to scuba dive. She decided to study ocean plants and concentrated on the study of algae.

Scientists underwent extensive training above ground before their 10-day mission in Tektite, the underwater research laboratory.

Sylvia completed a PhD at Duke University, and in 1970 led a team of female scientists as part of the Tektite II project, exploring the coral reefs and wildlife on the ocean floor off the Virgin Islands. The team also studied the physical effects of life underwater on the human body. The project was a success, and Sylvia became a celebrity. She was invited to give talks about ocean life and exploration.

In 1979, Sylvia made the deepest scuba dive then made by a woman. She reached the ocean floor at a depth of 1,250 feet (381 meters). In the 1980s, she reached the bottom of Crater Lake, Oregon, in a one-person submarine. The lake is 1,500 feet (457 m) deep. In 1982, Sylvia cofounded a company called Deep Ocean Engineering to explore the deep oceans.

Sylvia's work creating protected ocean areas, such as the Monterey Bay National Marine Sanctuary, helps harbor seals and other ocean animals to breed in safety.

Sylvia has been involved in protecting the waters around the United States, and has won awards for her conservation work. One of her areas of expertise is in minimizing environmental damage caused by oil spills. She was involved in cleanups after the *Exxon Valdez* and *Mega Borg* oil tanker accidents in 1989 and 1990, and also after the *Deepwater Horizon* offshore oil rig disaster in 2010.

In 2009, Sylvia won a TED—Technology, Entertainment, Design—award and used the prize money she was given to found Mission Blue. The organization aims to create marine protected areas worldwide. These areas are called "Hope Spots." By 2018, 94 Hope Spots had been set up, from polar regions to the equator.

The oceans of the world cover about **320,000,000,000** **cubic miles** (1,332,000,000 cubic kilometers).

The **National Marine Sanctuary System** has 14 protected areas that cover more than **783,000 square miles** (2,003,000 sq km) of ocean.

Mission Blue aims to protect **20 PERCENT** of the world's oceans by 2020.

Hope Jahren

Name: Anne Hope Jahren
Born: 1969, Austin, Minnesota
Occupation: Geobiologist
Education: University of Minnesota, University of California, Berkeley
Major discoveries and achievements: Analyzed ancient trees on Axel Heiberg Island, identified release of methane hydrates 117 million years ago, author of the book *Lab Girl (2016)*
Major honors: Leopold Leadership Fellow, 2011; Australian Society for Medical Research Medallist, 2018

Hope Jahren studied geology at the University of Minnesota. She gained her PhD in soil science at the University of California, Berkeley. Her study used **isotopes** to investigate what had happened to plants millions of years ago. Using the same techniques, Hope studied fossilized plants to identify changes in Earth's atmosphere. She was able to demonstrate that there had been an increase in the release of methane hydrates 117 million years ago. Methane can cause big changes in the atmosphere. From 1999, Hope studied the remains of ancient trees on Axel Heiberg Island, in the Canadian Arctic.

Global warming has caused the frozen ground in the Siberian tundra to start melting. This has released large quantities of methane into the atmosphere.

The remains of the trees on Axel Heiberg are unusual. They have not fossilized into stone as is usual with fossils. Because of the cold, dry climate, the trees had been **mummified**. This made them easier to examine and gave Hope more information than she would normally have learned from fossils. She was able to work out what the environment might have been like on the island 45 million years ago.

These were important results. Finding out what happened to Earth in the past may hold clues about what might happen in the future. The effects of the release of methane over millions of years ago might be reproduced again soon. Methane deposits in arctic **permafrost**, particularly in Siberia, are warming up and the once-frozen methane is being slowly released. Scientists are not sure what effect this will have on the planet. Looking at Hope's research into the atmosphere and plants long ago gives scientists a better idea of what may happen to Earth in the future.

Hope wrote a book, *Lab Girl*, in 2018. It describes her life growing up in a scientific family, and how she eventually became a scientist. She describes the problems of obtaining grants and funding. She also describes how hard it can be to find a university or study center that is prepared to encourage student scientists to follow their own, independent lines of research.

Hope made a groundbreaking study of the trees on Axel Heiberg Island. These trees are well preserved because, when they fell, they were covered with fine dust. As the Arctic froze over, the cold, dry climate stopped the wood from rotting.

Methane is dangerous. It traps **84 times** more heat in the atmosphere than **carbon dioxide.**

Rice fields produce **110 million tons** (100 million metric ton) of **methane** gas per year.

The trees on **Axel Heiberg Island** grew **115 feet** (35 m) tall and lived for **1,000** years.

Timeline of Life Science

From the seventeenth century onward, women played an important part in the emerging life sciences. Their discoveries helped to develop further understanding of the world, and added to scientific knowledge. By the 1900s, women were making groundbreaking discoveries in all branches of the life sciences. In the 2000s, women continue to be at the forefront of research that is changing the way people think about and relate to the planet.

1700 | 1800 | 1850 | 1900 | 1940

1699
German naturalist Maria Sibylla Merian visits South America to catalog the plants and insects.

1702
Catherine Jérémie settles in the French-Canadian colony of Montreal. She sends plants back to France for classification.

1823
Mary Anning discovers a complete plesiosaur dinosaur skeleton.

1848
Scientist Mary Ann Whitby helps Charles Darwin by giving him information on how silkworms reproduce.

1930
Barbara McClintock describes how chromosomes have a cross-shaped interaction when they divide.

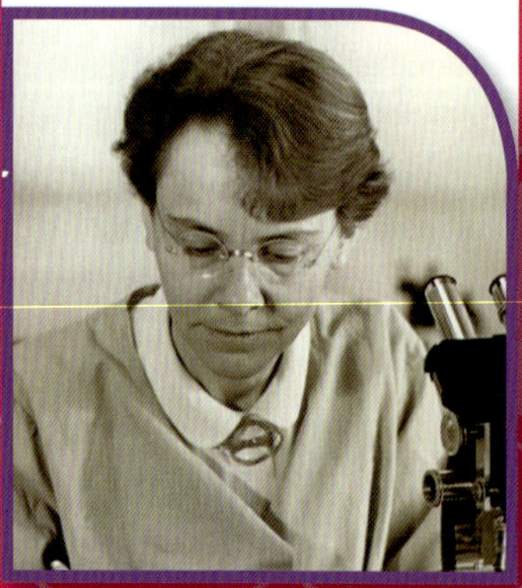

Spinner dolphins are one of the species protected by Sylvia Earle's National Marine Sanctuary program.

1960 1990 2000 2010 2019

1962
Rachel Carson publishes *Silent Spring*.

1967
Dian Fossey sets up the Karisoke Research Center to study mountain gorillas in Rwanda.

1990
Sue Hendrickson discovers the most complete skeleton of a *Tyrannosaurus rex* ever found. It is named "Sue" for her.

2009
Sylvia Earle founds the Mission Blue organization, which helps to protect the marine environment.

2017
Hope Jahren's book *Lab Girl* wins the American Association for the Advancement of Science prize for Excellence in Science.

2019
Fifty-nine percent of the students taking biology and biomedical courses in the U.S. are women.

Quiz

1 What does a palaeontologist study?

2 What was a plesiosaur?

3 What is cytogenetics?

4 What did Barbara McClintock study with new, powerful microscopes?

5 Who did Rachel Carson write radio scripts for?

6 What was the name of Rachel Carson's book on the effects of pesticides?

7 Who set up a research center for studying mountain gorillas in Rwanda in 1967?

8 What was the Tektite II Project?

9 What are "Hope Spots"?

10 Who wrote *Lab Girl*?

ANSWERS

1. Living things that died out millions of years ago **2.** A large seawater reptile that lived in the Jurassic period **3.** The study of how genes affect a cell **4.** Chromosomes **5.** The Bureau of Fisheries **6.** *Silent Spring* **7.** Dian Fossey **8.** An underwater research project off the Virgin Islands **9.** Protected areas of the ocean **10.** Hope Jahren

Key Words

botany: the study of plants

cell: the smallest unit of life

chromosomes: structures found in all cells, which carry the genes that pass on characteristics

conservationists: people who work to protect living things from harm

ecosystems: a community of interacting organisms and their physical environment

evolution: a change in the characteristics of a living thing over generations

food chain: a series of organisms that are each dependent on the next as a source of food

fossils: the preserved remains of plants or animals

geneticists: scientists who study genetics, the branch of science that studies the role that genes play in passing traits between organisms

geologist: a scientist who studies Earth's history through its rocks and rock formations

herbivores: animals that feed on plants

isotopes: atoms that have a different number of neutrons compared to other atoms of the same substance

microbiologists: scientists who study microscopic organisms

mummified: dried up and preserved

mutations: changes in the genetic material of a cell

naturalist: an expert in natural history

natural selection: the process by which a species changes over time in response to changes in the environment

oceanographer: a scientist who studies the oceans and the plants and animals that live in them

permafrost: thick layer of soil that remains below freezing point all year round

pesticides: chemicals used to kill insects that harm crops

poaching: illegal hunting

radioactive: emitting a powerful and dangerous form of energy

species: a class of plants or animals that have the same main characteristics

taxonomy: the science of naming, defining, and classifying groups of organisms

Index

Published by Smartbook Media Inc.
350 5th Avenue, 59th Floor New York, NY 10118
Website: www.openlightbox.com

Project Coordinator: Heather Kissock
Art Director: Terry Paulhus

Library of Congress Control Number: 2019942200

ISBN 978-1-5105-4428-4 (hardcover)
ISBN 978-1-5105-4429-1 (multi-user eBook)

Printed in Guangzhou, China
1 2 3 4 5 6 7 8 9 0 23 22 21 20 19

072019
311218

Photo Credits
Every reasonable effort has been made to trace ownership and to obtain permission to reprint copyright material. The publisher would be pleased to have any errors or omissions brought to its attention so that they may be corrected in subsequent printings.

The publisher acknowledges Alamy, iStock, Dreamstime, Shutterstock, and Wikimedia as its primary image suppliers for this title.